Do you know . . .

A library is a magic castle with many Word Windows in it?

What is a Word Window?

If you answered, "A book," you're right.

A book is a Word Window because the words, and the pictures that tell about the words, let you look and see many things. Books are your windows to the wide, wide world around you.

A Pocketful of Pets

by Jane Belk Moncure
illustrated by Linda Hohag
and Lori Jacobson

Published by
THE CHILD'S WORLD ®

Mankato, Minnesota

The Library —
A Magic Castle

Come to the magic castle
When you are growing tall.
Rows upon rows of Word Windows
Line every single wall.
They reach up high,
As high as the sky,
And you want to open them all.
For every time you open one,
A new adventure has begun.

Mike opens a Word Window.
Guess what Mike sees?

A mama kangaroo.

"Please help me find Little Kangaroo," Mama says. "It is time for his nap."

"I will help you," says Mike.

Just then a puppy comes by.

"Please help us find Little Kangaroo.
It is time for his nap," says Mike.

Puppy looks in a . . .

doghouse.

Little Kangaroo is not there.
Puppy looks and looks until he

gets so sleepy, he hops into Mama Kangaroo's pocket. Just then . . .

. . . a kitten
comes by.

"Please help us find Little Kangaroo.
It is time for his nap," says Mike.

Kitten looks in a tree.

Little Kangaroo is not there. Kitten looks and looks until she gets . . .

so sleepy, she hops into Mama
Kangaroo's pocket.

Just then a duck comes by.

"Please help us find Little Kangaroo.
It is time for his nap," says Mike.

Duck looks in the pond. He looks
and looks until he gets so sleepy,

he hops into Mama Kangaroo's
pocket. Just then . . .

. . . two little lambs come by.

"Please help us find Little Kangaroo.
It is time for his nap," says Mike.

The lambs look in the barn.

Is Little Kangaroo there?

The lambs look and look until they
get so sleepy, they hop . . .

into Mama Kangaroo's pocket. Next . . .

. . . four little bunnies come by.

"Help us find Little Kangaroo. It is time for his nap," says Mike.

The little bunnies look in a field.
One bunny finds a butterfly.

One finds a grasshopper.

One bunny finds a mouse.

One finds a daisy.

But no one finds Little Kangaroo. The bunnies look until they get so sleepy.

What do they do?

Now Mama Kangaroo's pocket is full.

At last they come to the zoo. Guess who is at the zoo?

Little Kangaroo is crying for his mama.

So Mama Kangaroo gives Mike her pocketful of pets,

and Little Kangaroo climbs in for his nap!

Mike plays with the pets until
it is time to . . .

close the Word Window.

You can read these words with Mike.

kitten

duck

bunny

puppy

lamb

You can read more words with Mike.

cat

dog

hamster

turtle

goldfish

bird